COLORING BOOK

ALL ABOUT HORSES FOR KIDS

Coloring book. All abour Horses for Kids. Cooolz Ltd., 2019. 40 p., illustrated.

ISBN 978-9934-8711-9-1

Dear friends!

The horse is one of the most beautiful and graceful animals in the world. This book will tell you about the ancestors and relatives of the horse we know today. You will learn how the horse has been living by man's side for centuries, helping him to work, to fight, and to travel.

You will get to know a variety of horse breeds: the most beautiful and the fastest, the biggest and the smallest. You will discover the exciting world of equestrian sports, and the different kinds of equestrian activities and their rules. You will learn about some interesting equestrian games and unusual competitions practiced by different nations.

This book will also teach you how to take care of a horse. You will find out what clothes and gear are used in equestrian sports, how horses can treat people and keep them healthy, and many more interesting things.

The history of the horse began sixty million years ago. In the dense forests of America, there lived an animal known as **Eohippus**. It was the size of a dog and did not look much like a horse at all. It had an arched back, a long tail, and toes instead of hooves: four on the front legs and three on the hind. After millions of years of evolution, the Anchitherium appeared. It was bigger (about the size of a pony) and was good at running on its strong legs, which had three toes on each foot.

As the climate changed, forests gave way to steppes, which are wide open grassy plains. This had an effect on the animals' evolution, because they needed to adjust to living on dry and solid ground. This was when the Hipparion, an animal somewhat like today's gazelle, appeared.

And around five million years ago, there appeared the Pliohippus. Though it had no hooves yet, it had one strong toe instead of three, and had more in common with the horses we know today.

From America, these animals migrated to Europe, Asia, and Africa. In Latin, scientists call the contemporary horse (the strong and beautiful animal from the Perissodactyla order) Equus Ferus.

Three thousand five hundred years ago, the King of Cyprus wrote to the Pharaoh of Egypt: "I wish good health to you, your family and your horses." The greeting would have come as no surprise to the pharaoh, as the horse was a respected animal, a loyal servant of military commanders. The horse made a successful military career in Ancient Egypt, and thanks to them, the army became powerful and mobile.

The Egyptians began using chariots in the sixteenth century BC. The vehicles played a critical role on the battlefield. The driver controlled the four horses that pulled the two-wheeled chariot, and he held a shield to protect the sharpshooting archer. One chariot could replace 100 foot soldiers. The largest battle in ancient history (Battle of Kadesh, 1299 BC) involved five thousand chariots. In a harness, horses could gallop at speeds of up to 25 miles per hour (40 km/h), which was the speed record at that time. The pharaohs were famous for their love of fast rides: In the tomb of Tutankhamun, six chariots were found.

When speaking of a hardworking person, we sometimes say that he or she is a willing horse. This comparison is not random. Strong, tough, and resilient, the horse is a true worker. In the eighteenth century, horsepower (hp) was recognized as a unit of measurement. Horsepower is used to measure the power of engines in cars, motorcycles, and tractors.

Meanwhile, one-horsepower equipment has been working in agriculture for several thousand years. Horses were used to pull ploughs, harrows, or seed drills. Horses adapt easily to various climates and working in the toughest conditions. To get the maximum power, scientists selected special breeds. For instance, the best horse for agricultural work in mountainous areas is a pony.

Steam and gas-operated tractors and combines, which eventually replaced horses in agriculture, were invented only in the late nineteenth century. But even today, some farmers continue to work with horses. Horsepower is environmentally friendly. And, moreover, the farmer's horse is more than just a worker: he is a friend.

The horse has always been man's loyal friend and assistant, his breadwinner and pride. Most of the time, horses were used for riding. Archaeological findings show that horses were put into harness three to four thousand years BC.

Horses played an important role in trading. Horse-driven wagons were used for traveling and trading with neighboring countries. The first wagons were wooden carts, pulled by strong horses along rough tracks.

Genghis Khan's successor, Kublai Khan, established the first horse-driven cargo service back in the thirteenth century; his network covered the whole empire. Later, the first post service appeared in Europe. The strongest and fastest horses were selected to carry the letters and parcels.

As people learned how to build good roads, they also improved carts. In the fifteenth century, the carriage appeared. A beautiful carriage became a must-have vehicle for a wealthy man. Rich people would have nine to twelve horses hitched to their carriages, which were upholstered with velvet and furs; the wheels were plated with silver.

In the sixteenth century, the first horse-driven intercity transport, the stagecoach, appeared. In the nineteenth century, the horse-pulled railway was created; the railway car pulled by two horses was a precursor of today's trams. The predecessor of the motor bus was the omnibus, a horse-drawn coach that could carry fifteen to twenty passengers.

The horse remains the symbol of grace and speed in the automotive industry. Logos with horses adorn the bonnets of the luxury racing and sport cars Ferrari, Porsche, and Ford Mustang.

The circus is a magic world of lights, music, and fairy tales that brings joy to children and adults alike. And this world employs many horses. The first equestrian circus appeared in the eighteenth century when a British cavalryman named Philip Astley returned from war, opened a riding school, and started doing performances. The riders did amazing acrobatic tricks on horseback, to the delight of crowds of spectators.

The diameter of every circus arena is 42.7 feet (13 m). This never changes because it is the best size for horses. Acrobatic tricks require the horse's back to be tilted toward the center of the arena at the same angle. The ring's barrier must be a convenient height for a horse to put his front hooves on and continue running around the arena with his hind legs. All the most spectacular acts of the horse show—the pirouette, gambado, levade—are the high school airs.

Don't worry if you see a man with a whip in the arena. He does not use the lunge whip to punish the horse but uses it as a pointer to instruct the horse what to do next. The trainer acts like an orchestra conductor, and the lunge whip is his or her baton. The horse understands many signs, invisible to the audience, that make us believe that the horse dances or gets on his hind legs of his own will. For a good performance, the actor horses are rewarded with a treat and a sweet word.

There are around 300 breeds of these beautiful animals in the world, and each one is unique. Some horse breeds have been known to humankind since ancient times, but the majority of them were bred in the eighteenth and nineteenth centuries. Every time, the breeders were driven by a certain target: Some breeds are better at carrying cargo, and others are prizewinning racers.

Horses are divided into groups by a number of features: origin, purpose, place of habitat, and selection methods. Each breed can be included in this or that group based on different features, which is often seen in the name: American Saddlebred, Australian Half-Breed, Brazilian Sport Horse, Russian Heavy Draught.

The fastest horse breed in the world is the **Thoroughbred**. Not so long ago, it was known as the English Thoroughbred, but after the breed spread around the world, the name was changed. Thoroughbreds are bred to race. They have a muscular body, long legs, and a big heart that can weigh up to 13.2 pounds (6 kg) and works like a powerful engine. A good Thoroughbred can reach 40.3 miles per hour (65 km/h). Different breeds may take part in racing, but Thoroughbreds are in the league of their own. Thoroughbreds do not compete with any other breeds.

The second-fastest horse breed is the **Arabian**. According to legend, Allah took a handful of the South Wind, blew His breath over it, and created a horse to be as fast as the wind. In one hour, the Arabian horse can cover 37.2 miles (60 km).

Just look at the beautiful Arabian horses holding their heads high! The specific refined profile of the head, huge black eyes, high-set tail, thick mane, regal grace, and hot blood make up the portrait of a true Arabian horse. They come in a variety of colors but are always solid colored. This is not just a beautiful horse: The severe desert climate made it tough and enduring. The breed was developed by the Bedouins in the fourth to fifth centuries in the Arabian Peninsula. Today, Arabian horses have the world at their feet.

The third fastest breed is the French Thoroughbred, which can achieve a speed of 31 miles per hour (50 km/h).

Other fast horse breeds include the Russian, American, French, and Orlov trotters.

All horses are incredibly beautiful. But three breeds are recognized as the most beautiful in the world: the Akhal-Teke, the Arabian, and the Friesian.

The Akhal-Teke is the most ancient of the Thoroughbreds, developed around 5000 years ago. They cannot be confused with any others as they are easy to recognize by the long lines that distinguish their build. These are tall horses (around 63 inches [160 cm] at the withers) with long legs, back, and neck, and almond-shaped eyes. The build of the Akhal-Teke is often compared to that of a sighthound or a cheetah. They can be of various colors, including bay, black, chestnut, or grey. They are distinguished with a typical gold or silver sheen to their coats.

The **Friesian** horse is the so-called "black gold" of the Netherlands, the most beautiful of the draught breeds (developed in the sixteenth to seventeenth centuries). Friesians are also known as the "black pearls," because the stallions are always black. The mares may have a small white star on the forehead, the size not exceeding 1.18 inches (3 cm). The Friesian is large, strong, and elegant with a beautiful arched neck, long mane and tail, and "feathers" (long thick hair) over their black hooves. These horses are famous for their striking appearance and friendly character.

The most ancient of the living breeds is **Przewalski's horse** (named after the Russian geographer who discovered them). People have never succeeded in domesticating this wild horse. It resists any attempts at training or breaking-in (learning to be ridden or driven). In appearance, they combine some features of a horse and a donkey. They are short and stocky, with a ridged mane and a wide long tail. In the Asian deserts where Przewalski's horses used to live, they haven't been seen for over fifty years. Perhaps they have become extinct in the wild. Now they can be only found in wildlife sanctuaries and zoos.

The biggest horse breeds are strong and powerful heavy draught horses. The most commonly known are the Shire and Percheron breeds. They descend from medieval battle horses. In those times, horses had to carry some really heavy loads. A knight's armor weighed 132 pounds (60 kg), and then the weight of the knight himself, plus the weight of the horse's own armor. Only the strongest and biggest horses could carry such weight on their backs.

An English successor of the medieval knights' horses is the **Shire** draught horse. All representatives of this breed are big (up to 72.8 inches [185 cm] at the withers) and weigh over 2204 pounds (1000 kg). In 1846, the biggest horse in the world was registered, a stallion called Sampson. This champion was 86.6 inches (220 cm) at the withers and weighed 3351 pounds (1520 kg). No wonder he was nicknamed Mammoth. Shires may be a little slow, but they are very strong. One horse can pull an airplane weighing two to three tons. Among their characteristics are a white face and white half-stockings, often on the hind legs only.

France also has its strong horse: the **Percheron**. This breed is recognized as the most graceful of the draughts, as it has a good share of Arabian blood. The Percheron impresses with its might and harmony. The horse is big but not heavy-set. The height can reach 68.9 inches (175 cm) at the withers. The most typical color is grey, but they can also be black. Percherons are very responsive horses, patient and easy to train.

Even though replaced by trucks, draught horses are still popular. One can often see them at equestrian trade exhibitions and shows in Europe. In England, Shires march proudly at every parade, triumphantly pulling the mobile billboards.

Ponies are small horses. Among them, some are not taller than 31.5 inches (80 cm), and some are quite big animals, up to 57 inches (145 cm) tall. Yes, ponies are small, but they are also strong and sturdy. These equines have an impressive life expectancy. For an ordinary horse, thirty years old is an extreme age, while a pony can live to fifty.

There are around twenty pony breeds. The most famous are the Shetland, Scottish, and Welsh ponies. Shetlands are tough. This miniature draught horse has short, sturdy legs; a stocky body; a thick coat; and a thick mane and tail. They used to work in mines. In the course of a year, these little toilers walked about 3,000 miles (5000 km) underground, carrying about 3000 tons of coal.

Today, ponies work in parks and horse-riding schools and take part in sporting competitions. They give children a ride on their back or pull them in carts. With their help, children learn the basics of horseback riding. A five-to-seven-year-old child can easily ride a pony, and falling from its back is not painful or scary. Moreover, ponies are very friendly. They begin to trust you after you have spent about an hour with it.

One of the smallest ponies in the world is the Falabella miniature horse. It is often confused with a pony, though it is not the same. The height of the Falabella ranges from 15.7 to 29.5 inches (40 to 75 cm). Only the smallest children, aged from three to five years old, can ride one. Sometimes these ponies even share houses with people.

According to Hippocrates, there are four basic horse coat colors: grey, bay, chestnut, and black. The rest of the colors are considered to be their derivatives: pinto, spotted, skewbald, palomino, roan, dun, grullo. For some horse breeds, a wide color range is allowed, whereas for others the range of colors may be strictly limited.

The **Appaloosa** developed in the United States and is known for its unusual color. It is spotted: The horse is "sprinkled" with oval-shaped spots, a little like a leopard skin or a Dalmatian. This horse can be either dark with light spots, or almost white with dark spots. Interestingly, it is not just the coat that is mottled, but also the skin, and the hooves are striped. A spotted horse always attracts a lot of attention.

Some horse breeds have already disappeared, and some are on the brink of extinction. The rarest breed is the **Sorraia**. There are only 200 left in the world. These shaggy little horses used to live in the wilds, until in 1920 a zoologist found a herd in Portugal, near the Sorraia river. The adult horses are a beautiful dun color with a silver sheen. The little foals have stripes all over, reminiscent of zebra stripes. Interestingly, the Sorraia remained unknown until the twenty-first century. Portugal placed the horses under protection.

The horse has quite a few relatives: the zebra, donkey, onager, mule, and hinny. Let us get to know some of them better.

The **donkey** was domesticated long ago, around 4000 years BC. A wild donkey is rare today; there are not more than 200 left. They are considered an endangered species and are under protection. Strongly built, the donkey is a cute animal. It is not as tall as the horse. Its coat is grey, black, or brown, with a dark stripe along the back. The donkey has a short mane and a tail with a tassel. The donkey's ears are longer than the horse's and gives the animal excellent hearing. However, its voice is horrible, and even more so because donkeys like performing altogether. Once one of them has cried its "hee-haw," the others join in immediately.

The donkey is strong and sturdy. It can work for ten hours a day, pulling loads exceeding its own weight. This patient animal can go without water for a long time and is easy to keep. Usually calm and friendly, the donkey will bravely defend its foal from a dog or a fox. Donkeys are often accused of being stubborn. But this is not true. In fact, the donkey simply knows its limits. When it's tired, it stops to rest and won't move, no matter what. History does not tell of a single donkey that died of exhaustion. When treated with care, donkeys become very loyal to their owners.

A scientist once called the **zebra** "a horse of the sun, reminiscent of a tiger" due to its striped coat. But here is a question: Is the zebra white with black stripes or vice versa? Scientists have come to the conclusion that it is black, with each zebra having its unique white pattern. Zebra foals use the stripes to recognize their mother. The baby zebras' stripes are brownish. Half an hour after birth, the little foals begin to walk and drink milk. Zebra milk is not white, but pink. Zebras are family animals; many of them mate for life. Large herds are usually divided into small families.

When most of the zebras in a herd are resting, several "volunteers" stay alert to warn the others in case of danger. People have tried to domesticate the zebra but have never succeeded. They are timid animals; even at the zoo, they run away if anyone approaches their enclosure.

Equestrian sport is very diverse. However, only three disciplines are included in the Olympic Games: dressage, three-day eventing, and show jumping.

Show jumping is a spectacular sport, with many varieties of competitions. A course with ten to sixteen jumps (different obstacles and water ditches) up to 6.56 feet (2 m) high or wide is laid out. A bell rings to signal each competitor to begin. The course must be covered within the set time. Penalty points are collected for exceeding the time limit, the number of jumps knocked down, falls, and refusals to jump. If a horse and rider take twice the time limit to complete the course, the participant is disqualified from the competition. The rider with the fewest penalties wins. To win, both the horse and rider must not only be well-trained but also brave, decisive, and athletic.

Dressage is a competition that highlights the most advanced and refined riding skills. It is often compared to ballet on horseback. The horses demonstrate how they can move at different speeds and gaits (various ways in which a horse can move: walk, trot, and canter). The rider demonstrates his or her horse-riding skills. Each element of the competition leads on from the previous, with no rest in between.

Olympic dressage is held in a 66-by-198-feet (20-by-60-m) arena. The horses complete their routine, moving in straight and diagonal lines, as well as around the arena, and the judges are seated around the arena, watching the participants from all possible angles. Scores are based on the accuracy and grace of each required movement of the assigned test and rated on a scale of 0 to 10.

Three-day eventing is the most complicated of the three competitions. It is held over three days and consists of three disciplines: cross-country jumping, dressage, and show jumping. Eventing is the supreme test of the skill, versatility, courage, and endurance of horse and rider.

Racing can be on the flat or with jumps included on the racecourse. Thoroughbreds are exclusively used for this sort of racing, due to their exceptional speed.

Trotting races are confined to trotters, who compete in speed. Trotters first start racing at two years old and finish their racing career at the age of eight to twelve. The horses are prepared for a saddle trot race or harness racing. For harness racing, a two-wheeler sulky, reminiscent of a chariot, is used. It is very light, weighing around 25 pounds (11 kg). In a harness or under a saddle, the horse is controlled by a jockey. The jockey's skills are among the main factors of success.

A race between trotters at a hippodrome is called a heat. In different countries, horses compete at different distances. In the United States, the course is one mile (1609 m) whereas in Europe the distances are longer. The horse must maintain a clear trot throughout the race. A change in gait is a serious error; the trotter is announced to have committed a faulty action and gets disqualified from the race.

A racing horse is evaluated based on the prize money he has won. Outstanding prize-winning horses are extremely valuable.

Polo has been referred to as "the sport of kings and the king of sports." The game is over two thousand years old. It is a spectacular and expensive sport.

How is a polo match played? The match is played by two opposing teams of four riders and polo ponies. The players gallop their horses around the field, using a long-handled wooden mallet to try and hit a small hard ball between the opposing team's goalposts. There are no goalkeepers. The match consists of four to eight chukkas (periods) of seven minutes each, with a break of three minutes between chukkas. During the break, the players get on fresh horses.

Not every horse can endure such an intensive game. The polo pony is a special breed developed for this sport. They have great acceleration, can stop quickly, and can turn fast, all desirable abilities for a game where you never know where the ball may be in a second. Some polo ponies get even more excited about the game than their riders. Sometimes, the pony hits the ball through the goalposts with a kick of his hoof. To the amusement of the audience, these pony goals count.

The history of horse breeding in America is truly remarkable. Native Americans were among the best horse riders in the world. It seems like they had known horses for millennia, but this is not so. In prehistoric times, some horses were on the continent, but they became extinct during the Ice Age. In the sixteenth century, some domesticated horses were brought to the continent by colonists.

Native Americans captured some horses during battles and soon learned to control their horses with their legs and hips while their hands were busy holding their bows. Horses were used for bison hunting and equestrian games and were sources of great pride for Native Americans.

Many of the imported horses got away from people. Some lost their riders in battles, and some strayed from the herd while grazing. This is where the famous mustangs come from. The word mustang comes from the Spanish word mestengo, "a wild animal having no master." Huge herds of mustangs roamed the prairies; by the turn of the twentieth century, there were around two million. People began hunting mustangs and almost killed them off. Today, there are only ten to twenty thousand animals living in wildlife sanctuaries.

The cowboy is a symbol of America. Cowboys are agile, brave, and skillful horseback riders. Since the nineteenth century, cowboy has been used to refer to animal herders. In their free time, cowboys used to compete against each other in bronc riding, roping, and horse training. With time, the games acquired more rules and became what we call Western sports.

The most exciting Western sport is **rodeo**, which is riding a bucking horse or bull. Breaking in a wild mustang was normally the first thing the cowboy would do, and this is the skill today's rodeo is based on. To make the horse buck, a special belt is tied around his body while the horse is in a tight stall. The cowboy mounts the horse. The gates open, and out comes the rider on a bucking horse. To win, the rider must stay mounted for eight seconds. Rodeo participants dress like real cowboys: a checked shirt, leather "leggings" (chaps) over jeans, boots and, of course, a cowboy hat. Rodeo is a spectacular event enjoyed not only in the United States but across the world.

Japan still maintains a traditional combat sport of the samurais—**yabusame**, or traditional mounted archery.

A yabusame archer wearing a national costume gallops down a 278-yard-long track (255 m) at high speed toward the target. He must fire at and hit the target on the run. The archer controls the galloping horse mainly with his knees. The most challenging thing for him is to keep balance.

The targets are fixed at a height of 6.56 feet (2 m). The yabusame arrow is blunt in order to make a louder sound when it strikes the board. The explosion created by the strike is traditionally believed to transfer the archer's courage to the spectators. The judge stands by the target to give a signal when it is hit. He waves his fan and announces, "Target hit!" This spectacular event is over eight hundred years old. But yabusame is more than just a sport; it is an ancient national ritual. According to legend, the emperor hit three targets on horseback to propitiate the gods and pray for peace, wealth, and prosperity for his country.

Europe has kept the tradition of the **knights' tournament** since the eleventh century. In the Middle Ages, the tournament was a grand event. The course, or tiltyard, was carefully chosen. Hundreds of knights and thousands of spectators would gather. Each knight did his best to demonstrate his martial prowess, the splendor of his armor, and the power of his battle horse. The tournaments were based on the code of chivalry. It was prohibited to strike below the belt or to attack from behind. It was not allowed to beat an unarmed opponent or to hurt his horse. Rule breakers could get fined or even imprisoned.

At first, knights would duel with their combat weapons and fight to death. By the fifteenth century, the tournaments had become a sporting competition, and combat weapons had been replaced with safer ones. This was when a new kind of equestrian sport called jousting was invented and played by two horsemen wielding wooden lances with blunted tips. The weight of a knight in armor could reach 308.6 pounds (140 kg). At the moment of collision, the horse could be galloping at 18.6 miles per hour (30 km). The force of the strike was very strong. The knight tilted from his saddle (knocked off his horse) would lose.

Participants in today's tournaments use the same armor and wear the same clothes as in the fifteenth century. Contemporary knights not only look like medieval knights, they also respect the code of chivalry. The battle horse will live for as long as these tournaments are held.

Good tack is needed to keep the horse under control and comfortable. Tack consists of these items:

Bridle (headpiece): a set of straps fitted on the horse's head.

Bit: a metal mouthpiece. Part of the bridle and attached to the reins. Pulling on the reins pulls at the bit and tells the horse to slow down or stop.

Reins: leather straps fixed to the ends of the bit. They are used to adjust the position of the horse's head and to direct his movements.

Saddle: used not only for the comfort of the rider but also to protect the horse's back. The saddle is fitted individually. A well-fitted saddle makes it easier for the horse to carry the rider.

Stirrups: metal pieces in which the rider places his feet. Stirrups are used when mounting and keeping balance while riding.

At competitions, riders must follow a strict dress code. Show jumping requires wearing white jodhpurs and a red or black riding coat. A riding hat is compulsory. For dressage, the rider wears white breeches, a long black riding coat, a shirt, and a top hat (sometimes, a jockey cap).

Horseback riding clothes are comfortable and elegant. Riding wear consists of riding boots, jodhpurs (breeches), and gloves. And, of course, a riding hat! But first things first.

A jockey cap (a helmet with a visor) is very important to ensure the jockey's safety. This smart-looking, light but strong headgear protects the rider from head trauma in case of a fall.

A riding coat is a beautiful jacket made of a strong fabric with a velvet collar. It gives the rider a very smart look.

Jodhpurs are tightly fitting trousers. They are designed to keep the rider comfortable while mounted on a moving horse; for this reason, they have special inserts on the inner knees and no seams that could rub the skin.

Riding boots always have a small heel to help keep the foot in the stirrup. Spurs, if worn, are attached to boots and are used to increase control over the horse. Spurs are different today from those used by knights and cowboys, and do not hurt the horse.

Gloves protect the rider's hands. They ensure a comfortable grip and prevent skin being chafed by the reins. Moreover, they look very elegant.

The basic food for the horse is **hay**. Horses must always have hay available to munch. Besides keeping them full, munching saves horses from boredom. Horses need small meals three or four times a day at regular times, as they get accustomed to a daily routine. Wait at least one hour after he has eaten before riding a horse. The horse needs to drink a lot; in twenty-four hours he consumes around 9.24 gallons (35 l) of water, and even more in summer. The water must be clean, and in winter it should also be warm enough not to freeze. From the point of view of the horse, hygiene is about rolling in the dust, then shaking it off and brushing against a tree. In the wild, horses enjoy water and mud baths. Basically, they do their best to take care of their appearance.

We like horses to be clean and shiny, too, showing off their health and well-being. Horses need brushing, and not only for the sake of beauty. If any dirt gets under the saddle, it can rub the skin and create painful sores.So, what do we need to clean the horse? A special tool kit: a brush, a comb, a hoof pick, and a couple of sponges. Brush the horse with a little pressure; make sure you are not tickling him but giving him a nice massage. The comb is used for the mane; the tail is cleaned manually, so as not to damage the fluffy beauty with a comb. The condition of his hooves is of utmost importance. Once they are worn out, the horse begins to limp. To protect hooves from cracking, they can be treated with a special cream. Horseshoes are used to keep hooves healthy. Every month and a half, a farrier replaces the horseshoes. At least once a year the horse is examined by a vet to make sure he is in good health.

Doctors say that the advantages of horseback riding are enormous. The horse is a living cross trainer!

A science called **hippotherapy** studies the ways to treat people with the help of horses. In many countries, there are horse barns attached to hospitals, to teach patients how to ride. Riding helps them regain their health.

On horseback, the rider makes a variety of moves he or she never does in everyday life. Rocking in three directions—up and down, left and right, back and forth—loads and relaxes the muscles at the same time. Moreover, it strengthens the hips and improves coordination and balance. And since the horse rider has to sit up straight, it also improves posture.

The body temperature of the horse is higher than that of man: up to 99–101°F (37.2–38.3°C). The rider's muscles are warmed by the horse. Moreover, the slight body tilting from the moving horse lightly massages the internal parts of the body.

Today, people spend too much time at the computer. In big cities, people hardly ever look into the distance, which may develop near-sightedness. Walking or riding in open spaces reduces the risk of this disorder.

Hippotherapy often helps children with disabilities. Children can ride horses in different positions: lying across the horse's back, sitting backward, lying on the horse and holding on to its neck. Moreover, the little rider can do special exercises. And sitting on such a big and strong animal, controlling it, helps the child gain self-confidence.

Horses can also remedy aggression and quick temper in adults. Stroking a horse or playing with his mane makes us feel positive emotions. Regular contact with horses is relaxing and soothing. The horse is a good doctor.

At first, horses may seem big and scary, but those who have ridden them at least once always say that it is awesome! The emotions one feels from meeting this beautiful animal makes it really worth finding the courage to approach a horse.

You may think you are ready to try an equestrian sport. But what about taking a leisure ride first? That feels like a real adventure! You need courage to get into the saddle and begin to stroll along paths. During the ride, you breathe fresh air and enjoy the view. It feels great to put video games and studies aside! Give in to the breeze in your face and the rustle of dry leaves under the hooves of your horse. Isn't it a perfect way to reset your mind?

It is so nice to make friends with an animal and feel its response. A horse can be just as friendly as a fluffy puppy! The best reward for a rider is the horse's trust, because you can never force him to do what he doesn't want to.

Treat your horse to a carrot, a sliced apple, or a piece of watermelon. When you approach your new friend with a treat, always hold it out on your open palm. Pat the horse on the neck in a friendly way every time you say hello or goodbye.

It is always exciting to spend time with experienced horse riders. These are people with strong characters. The first steps in any equestrian sport are never easy. Many times, they have fallen off the horse. Their first competitions were, perhaps, a failure. But despite all the challenges, they chose equestrian sport as their lifestyle. We can learn a lot from such people.

It is really worthwhile taking a horseback ride and asking yourself what it was like for you. It may be fun or a little scary, at first.

But it is fine to experience joy and fear at the same time.
The main thing is to try something new.
It is always a victory. Enjoy your ride!

CONTENTS

Coloring book. All abour Horses for Kids

Cooolz Ltd., 2019. 40 p., illustrated.

ISBN 978-9934-8711-9-1